# *The Grace and Grandeur of*
# NATCHEZ HOMES

Text and Illustrations by Joseph A. Arrigo
Photographs by Dick Dietrich with Rudi Holnsteiner

VOYAGEUR PRESS

# *The Grace and Grandeur of* NATCHEZ HOMES

**Library of Congress Cataloging-in-Publication Data:**
Arrigo, Joseph A. 1930–
The grace and grandeur of Natchez homes / by Joseph A. Arrigo.
p.   cm.
Includes bibliographical references and index.
ISBN 0-89658-226-4
1. Dwellings—Mississippi—Natchez. 2. Dwellings—Mississippi—
Natchez—Pictorial works. 3. Architecture, Domestic—Missis-
sippi—Natchez. 4. Architecture, Domestic—Mississippi—
Natchez—Pictorial works. 5. Natchez (Miss.)—Buildings, struc-
tures, etc. 6. Natchez (Miss.)—Buildings, structures, etc.—Picto-
rial works. I. Title.
F349.N2A77   1994
976.2'26—dc20                                    94-10729
                                                 CIP

Edited by Dee Ready
Printed in Hong Kong
96   97   98   5   4   3   2

**Published by Voyageur Press, Inc.**
P.O. Box 338, 123 North Second Street
Stillwater, MN 55082 U.S.A.
612-430-2210, fax 612-430-2211

**Please write or call, or stop by, for our free catalog of natural
history publications.** Our toll-free number to place an order or to
obtain a free catalog is 800-888-9653.

**Educators, fund-raisers, premium and gift buyers, publicists, and
marketing managers:** Looking for creative products and new sales
ideas? Voyageur Press books are available at special discounts when
purchased in quantities, and special editions can be created to your
specifications. For details contact our marketing department.

Photo on front cover: Stanton Hall. Photo on back cover: Monmouth
—gardens. Photo on page 1: Rosalie—floral arrangement in staircase window. Photo on page 3: The Wigwam—interior of home.

# Contents

CONTINUED

CONTINUED

# *Preface*

Geographic location and economics as well as the profound sense of history and personal dignity felt by the people of Natchez have left the structural treasures of this famous Mississippi city intact. Though not intended specifically as a guide, *The Grace and Grandeur of Natchez Homes* contains artistic and photographic depictions of many of Natchez's historic homes built before the American Civil War.

The abundance of historically significant and beautiful houses in Natchez made the selection criterion difficult. In fact, the text includes some of the lesser-known houses and excludes other perhaps more well-known homes because of the availability of the former to Dick Dietrich, the photographer. I hope no one takes offense if a "favorite" house does not appear in this book. Because almost every old structure in Natchez has historic value, recording and photographing each would be too monumental a task for the purposes of this book. Here I simply want to introduce the reader to some of the historical background and architectural beauty of thirty-nine of the old homes of Natchez.

I especially want to thank the 1932 Garden Club members who organized the first Natchez Pilgrimage, an event that opened many of the city's antebellum residences to the public. The Pilgrimage now features pageants, balls, lectures, and other social functions. Held both in the spring and in the fall, the Natchez Pilgrimage has grown to become probably the largest "industry" in this historic city along the Mississippi River. Its success has been the biggest motivating factor in the continuing restoration, maintenance, and interest in the city's grand architectural treasures of the pre-Civil War period.

In addition, I want to thank all those owners who patiently and graciously corrected any errors in my original manuscript. The goal of any writer of history is accuracy, and though notable historians wrote many of the references I consulted for this book, I still found these authors disagreeing about dates, names, and stories for these historical homes. Seemingly, history is more art than science.

My hope is that this book will serve either as a remembrance of your visit to Natchez, whose past is ever present, or as an inspiration to journey to this historic national jewel and see its treasures.

— **Joseph A. Arrigo**

MONTAIGNE — ENTRANCE AND STAIRCASE

EDGEWOOD — DINING ROOM

# Introduction

The Natchez Indians settled the fertile lands on the bluffs of the Mississippi River long before the early European explorers passed through what is now the city of Natchez. Because of the caste system among the Natchez Indians and because of their worship of the sun, some historians think that they were an offshoot of the Aztecs of Mexico.

Led by Hernando de Soto in 1541, the first Europeans to enter the general area were Spanish. Apparently, de Soto died within a year and his crew committed his remains to the Mississippi somewhere north of the site that would later become Natchez. The expedition explored what are now parts of Florida, Georgia, Alabama, Mississippi, Louisiana, and Arkansas.

More than a century after the ill-fated Spanish exploration, a French expedition entered the area. With Canada as his jumping-off point, Robert Cavelier, sieur de La Salle, descended the Mississippi in search of its mouth and a possible passage to Asia. In 1682, the Natchez Indian chief known as the Great Sun received La Salle and Henri de Tonti, his Italian lieutenant, and treated them as guests. As a result of this expedition, La Salle claimed all the land drained by the Mississippi as a territory of France and named it Louisiana after the French king. The explorer then returned to Europe to report his discoveries and to gain support for future expeditions.

Two years later, in 1684, La Salle returned to North America in an attempt to establish a colony. This time he explored along the coast of the Gulf of Mexico. Unsuccessful in his quest, La Salle was assassinated by mutinous men in his expedition when he landed somewhere on the Texas coast in 1687.

In 1699, Pierre le Moyne, sieur d'Iberville, explored the Mississippi Gulf Coast with his brother, Jean-Baptiste le Moyne, sieur de Bienville, and Tonti, the former lieutenant of La Salle. The three men and their party made their way up the Mississippi to the future site of Natchez. There they planned to establish a town on the commanding, easily defensible bluffs. In 1716, ten years after his brother's death, Bienville directed the Natchez Indians in the construction of Fort Rosalie, which he named after the wife of Pontchartrain, the French marine minister.

In 1729, the Natchez Indians attacked Fort Rosalie and massacred the garrison and colony, killing three hundred and taking several hundred women and slaves hostage as insurance against French reprisals. But over the next two years, the French retaliation almost annihilated the Indian tribe. By 1732, the tribal identity of the once powerful Natchez had been lost.

In 1762, after losing a seven-year war, France ceded the area called French Louisiana to Spain. In 1763, Spain in turn ceded to England the land east of the Mississippi River, except for the Isle of Orleans. In 1764, after several name and boundary changes, the Natchez district, including the settlement at Fort Rosalie, became a part of what was known as West Florida under British rule.

The British, eager to settle the area, awarded generous land grants to veterans of the Seven Years War, also called the French and Indian War. The American Revolution accelerated the development because the British offered land in West Florida to the Tories (pro-British colonists). This opportunity to es-

MONMOUTH — GARDENS

cape from the war to the north and to share in the generous land grant program brought many Tories to Natchez and gave the settlement a definite British flavor. Some of Mississippi's most noted and upstanding families were Tory settlers.

The British governing period, begun in 1763, lasted less than twenty years. In 1779, when Spain declared war on England due primarily to European considerations, Bernardo de Galvez, the Spanish governor of Louisiana in New Orleans, began to boldly occupy British posts from the outskirts of New Orleans all the way past Natchez. By 1782, Spain ruled all of West Florida.

Similar to the British governing period, the Spanish rule lasted only twenty years. At first, the Natchezians resented the Spanish officials, but the settlers soon learned to respect and even admire the efficiency of the Spanish governors. Manuel Gayoso de Lemos, later to serve as the last Spanish governor of Louisiana, assumed his post as governor of the Natchez district in 1789. Gayoso had his engineer, Señor Callel, plan the layout of the city in squares. During this period, the Spanish awarded even more land grants than the English had during their rule. Also during the Spanish regime, cotton became "king" because of improvements in transportation and because of Eli Whitney's invention of the cotton gin in 1793.

Soon most Natchez planters converted their fertile lands from indigo and tobacco, their primary crops, to the more profitable cotton. Plantation farmers developed new strains of cotton seeds and new methods of baling. In order to make cotton growing even more profitable, the plantation owners increased the number of slaves. Thus, the slave population, believed to be a necessary force to accommodate the labor-intensive planting, growing, harvesting, and producing of cotton, increased dramatically.

Because the newly formed United States exerted pressure on Spain to give up control of the Natchez region, the two countries signed a treaty in 1795, though the Spanish flag flew over Natchez until 1798. Spain agreed to withdraw below the thirty-first parallel. Thus, the United States now had access to the Mississippi River. With this treaty, Natchez became part of the Mississippi Territory, which comprised the lands now known as the states of Alabama and Mississippi. Just after the turn of the nineteenth century, the United States and the remaining Indian nations signed a treaty that opened Natchez to mail delivery and wagon trains.

Using the Natchez Trace, the first overland highway in the area, Americans flocked to Natchez. This migration created immediate growth in trade and culture. All classes of people were drawn to what was now the capital of a rich territory. The inauguration of steamboat service ushered in an era of abundance as Natchez became one of the great cotton ports of the world. Cotton planters, brokers, and the professionals who supported this agricultural industry amassed fabulous fortunes. As a result, a suave, sophisticated, aristocratic, and politically affluent community developed. According to some historians, in 1830 Natchez could count more millionaires among its population than any other U.S. city, except New York.

Wealthy Natchez planters began spending their money, building opulent, distinctive homes. They furnished these dwellings with elaborate, expensive furnishings. Unlike their Louisiana counterparts, Natchezians preferred the ambiance of town living, so instead of building their mansions on plantation grounds, they erected their extravagant homes in and about the city of Natchez, making it the center of their social, cultural, and commercial activity.

During this affluent period, however, another side of Natchez existed. "Natchez Under-the-Hill," an irregular shelf of batture (land built up by accumulated sediment) from the

LINDEN — BEDROOM

FAIR OAKS — ENTRANCE

Mississippi at the foot of the bluffs, was the city's waterfront. In the early days, the flatboats and keelboats carried not only cargo to and from the city but also rough and raffish crews. Catering to the desires of these men made the area a center of vice supposedly unequaled anywhere along the river. The waterfront in Natchez "out-sinned" even the notorious Gallatin Street in New Orleans.

Much of "Natchez-Under-the-Hill" has eroded and what remains today is a single street. Along it, visitors can see remnants of the old buildings, some of which have been restored as shops, restaurants, and bed-and-breakfasts. The area still comes alive, however, especially when the steamboats *Delta Queen* and *Mississippi Queen* dock there on their frequent visits. In 1991, the state voted to allow riverboat gambling in Natchez, so activity in this area most certainly will increase.

In 1817, Mississippi became the twentieth state of the Union, with Natchez as its capital. Shortly afterward, political forces moved the seat of government to the nearby town of Washington. But, within a few years, these same forces moved the capital to the city of Jackson, where it remains today.

Several setbacks affected the people of Natchez. Yellow fever, an almost always fatal viral disease, reached epidemic proportions all over the lower South (the last epidemic was in New Orleans in 1905). Though the outbreaks and other misfortunes during the middle years of the nineteenth century slowed the progress of Natchez, the city remained a rich agricultural center until the outbreak of the American Civil War. Fortunately the war did not destroy Natchez as it did many other Southern cities, including Jackson. The only military incident in Natchez occurred in 1863 when a Federal gunboat, the USS *Essex*, briefly shelled the town, causing slight damage. Federal troops marched into a virtually defenseless city and set up their headquarters at Rosalie, a beautiful house de-

scribed in the text. (Rosalie had been built on the site of Fort Rosalie, the first settlement.)

The Civil War completely overturned the social and economic structure of the area. With the freeing of the slaves and the economic depression that accompanied the war, Natchez citizens ceased building elaborate houses. The most outstanding victim of this situation was the sudden halting of construction on Longwood, a grand home featuring an eclectic blend of Italianate and Oriental-style architecture. Left in its unfinished state, Longwood clearly demonstrates the impact the Civil War had on the Natchez planting society and lifestyle. (This book contains the story of Longwood.)

After the Civil War ended, Natchez was generally better off than most other cities. Even though the Union army used many of the mansions as troop headquarters and hospitals and pastured its horses in the once magnificent gardens, the Natchez houses escaped serious damage.

After the war, the gradual loss of river traffic to the railroads thwarted the city's attempt at rebuilding her economy to prewar status. Left almost isolated from the rest of the country, Natchez became an almost forgotten city. Fortunes that had grown so rapidly in the early part of the century disappeared almost as fast. The owners of the great houses closed parts of their homes because they were too expensive to heat and maintain. Exteriors also suffered from the loss of maintenance, and each succeeding year took its toll on the historic mansions.

The banks that held the mortgages on the once grand homes had no choice but to allow the owners to continue living in them, doing what maintenance they could. Even when the South began to recover from the war, Natchez remained in its depressed state. Thus the Victorian architectural era, with its turrets and gingerbread, almost bypassed the city, simply because the citizens of Natchez could not afford to tear down,

THE PARSONAGE — BEDROOM

rebuild, and/or modernize. Ironically, this lack of prosperity preserved what the abundance of wealth had created.

Fortunately for all who have an interest in American lifestyles, Natchezians throughout the years have held on to their furnishings, paintings, china, mirrors, and other household accouterments. Thus, much of what the visitor to Natchez sees is original in these grand, graceful houses. And even with concessions to twentieth-century living, the city remains a picture of what life in Natchez was like when cotton was king.

❧ ❧ ❧

Early Natchez buildings were simple in design, utilizing locally available building materials. Most planters built their cottages with galleries in front and rear to provide shade from the hot sun and to allow the windows to remain open during the frequent summer rains. As the planters' fortunes increased, they began to construct more elaborate dwellings. The three primary styles of architecture and the years the styles began to come into fashion were as follows: Federal style—1800; Greek Revival—1833; and Italianate—1855. Of course, the architecture reveals some obvious crossover in both dates and styles.

In the first part of the nineteenth century, Americans adopted the Federal style from the English. This style features fanlights over entrance doors, oval windows, finely carved woodwork, and slender Roman columns. The dominant Federal-style homes in Natchez are Arlington, Auburn, Hawthorne, Linden, Mistletoe, Mount Repose, Rosalie, and Texada.

Historians credit the introduction of Greek Revival architecture to Natchez to the construction of the Agricultural Bank building in 1833. Within a short time, architects and builders were designing most new Natchez homes in the Grecian mode. This remained the dominant style until just before the Civil War when builders began to use Italianate designs, sometimes combining them with Greek Revival.

Greek Revival architecture emphasizes the solidity of the building. Its main features consist of Doric, Corinthian, or Ionic columns; rectangular openings; woodwork featuring wide, flat moldings; and large paneled doors. The ancient Greeks constructed their temples with large blocks of stone. To simulate this look, the Natchez builders used stucco extensively. They sometimes scored or painted the stucco to simulate the appearance of stone. The Burn, D'Evereux, Dunleith, and Monmouth are excellent examples of classic Greek architecture.

After 1855, buildings in Natchez began to show the influence of Italianate designs. For this style of architecture, designers copied the main features of Italian farm houses: buttressed cornices, extensive eaves, bay windows, arches, cast-iron ornamentation, towers, and stucco as the exterior wall covering. Though Italianate architecture came into favor at this time, builders almost always combined it with features of both Federal and Greek Revival styles. Thus, they created a somewhat distinctive architectural style.

Stanton Hall is probably the best example of this blend of styles. This palatial building, one of Natchez's finest, features four massive fluted Corinthian columns, supporting double galleries with wrought-iron grillwork balustrade in a rose design. The rectangular belvedere, a structure used as an observatory at the peak of the roof, displays large overhanging eaves. The exterior of Stanton Hall is completely stuccoed.

As the illustrations and photographs within this book show, Federal, Greek Revival, and Italianate detailing dominate Natchez's historical homes. Still, any Natchez visitor interested in architecture will be aware that some home builders did not simply follow popular trends. Instead, they borrowed from a variety of other styles.

MOUNT REPOSE — DINING ROOM

THE HOUSE ON ELLICOTT'S HILL —
SECOND-FLOOR GUEST SUITE

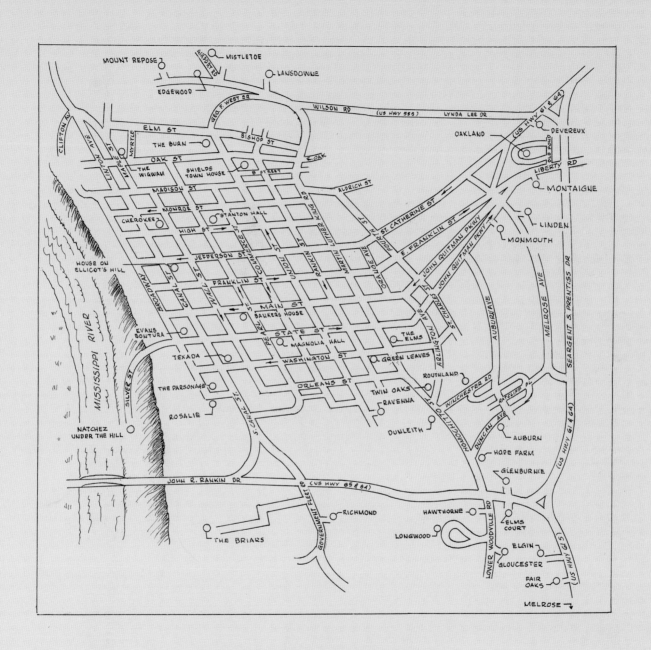

THE HOMES OF NATCHEZ
(map not drawn to scale)

# Auburn

In 1812, Judge Lyman G. Harding, Mississippi's first attorney general, asked Levi Weeks of Boston to design a home for him. Weeks had previously updated Cherokee and Gloucester (both featured in this book) by adding classic features to these older homes. However, his design of Auburn, a fine, red-brick building, was the first in the area to formally utilize the orders of classic architecture.

After the death of the Hardings, Dr. Stephen Duncan, originally from Carlisle, Pennsylvania, leased the house. Dr. Duncan married Margaret Ellis, whose affluent family lived in the area. When Mrs. Duncan died, Dr. Duncan sent their two children to the North for his sister to raise. In 1827, he purchased Auburn and married Catherine Bingham, a member of a wealthy and prominent Natchez family.

In the years that followed, Dr. Duncan amassed one of the largest fortunes in Natchez; he "owned" more than one thousand slaves. Interestingly, Dr. Duncan, although a major slaveholder, was philosophically opposed to the system and made no secret of his opposition to the establishment of the Confederacy, which was based primarily on the continuation of slavery.

With his associate, Dr. Ker of Linden, Dr. Duncan became involved in the famous legal battle concerning the will of their mutual friend, Captain Isaac Ross, who had requested that all his slaves be set free after his death. At that time, this request violated Mississippi law. The long, frustrating legal battle, which continued for years, was never clearly resolved. During the Civil War, Dr. Duncan left for the North in 1863 and never returned to Natchez.

Auburn originally measured sixty by forty-five feet with a thirty-one-foot-wide portico projecting out twelve feet. Its second owner, Dr. Duncan, added wings on each side of the house sometime after 1827. Service buildings at the rear of Auburn were formerly used as a kitchen, servants quarters, a carriage house, a billiard room, and cisterns.

Auburn's two-storied portico features four massive Ionic columns, which support the projecting pedimented roof. Side- and fan lights, both in a beautifully carved wooden framework, enhance Auburn's impressive entrance. The design of the fanlight surround is somewhat Egyptian in style.

The interior of this beautiful house features an entrance hallway that opens to a vaulted central hallway. Weeks designed all the rooms on the first floor for family living and entertainment. The second floor consists of four large bedrooms and two rooms now shown as a sitting room and a child's room. A most outstanding architectural feature in the house is an intricately devised freestanding, spiral stairway.

After Dr. Duncan moved to the North, Auburn remained unoccupied and fell into disrepair until 1911 when his descendants donated the house and several hundred acres of land to the city of Natchez for use as a public park. Duncan Park offers the people of Natchez many recreational facilities, including a golf course. The city has beautifully restored Auburn, which is open daily for tours. It is a National Historic Landmark property operated by the Auburn Garden Club.

AUBURN — ENTRANCE AND STAIRCASE

AUBURN — DINING ROOM

AUBURN — LIBRARY

21

# The Banker's House

This stuccoed Greek Revival town house served as a residence for a bank official of the adjoining First Bank of Commerce with which it shared a common wall. Built about 1837, the house contained a main bedroom supposedly located above the bank's storage vault. The custom of attaching a banker's residence to the bank itself was a heritage from the Spanish regime.

The front of The Banker's House faces Canal Street, and the bank building fronts on Main Street. Interestingly, the bank portion of the two buildings has also served as a U.S. Post Office, a National Guard Armory, and since 1946, the First Church of Christ Scientist. The Banker's House itself was, for a while, used as a rooming house. The notorious outlaws Jesse and Frank James once stayed there as overnight guests.

The two-story structure has a small portico that features two fluted Doric columns supporting a second, unroofed verandah. Wrought-iron railings grace both levels. The outstanding architectural feature in the interior of this fine house is the exquisitely carved woodwork surrounding the doors and windows. Black marble fireplace mantles also are attractive. Mr. and Mrs. Luther Stowers now live in The Banker's House and graciously open their home to the public during both spring and fall Pilgrimages. The house is also listed as a National Historic Landmark property.

# The Briars

This elaborate version of a planter's cottage stands on a high bluff overlooking the Mississippi River in an area that was once a suburb of Natchez. The Briars was probably built about 1812 or 1813, although no one knows the exact date.

Slender white Doric columns support a wide gallery across the front of this story-and-a-half house. Three entrance doors, one in the center of the house and one at each end, open to the gallery. Six large, symmetrically placed windows grace this front gallery. Four round-headed dormers protrude from the sloped, gable roof, and an unusual array of eight windows on the sides light the house at all levels.

The interior of The Briars, which is more spacious than would appear from the outside, is typical of most similar houses of the early nineteenth century. A wide central hall opens to large rooms on either side. The most outstanding architectural details of the house's interior consist of an unusual rounded Spanish ceiling in the central hallway, beautifully styled woodwork, and elaborate mantles. At the rear of the house is a large sun parlor, created from the later addition of a rear gallery. This beautifully designed room features a row of Spanish arches and two matching mahogany staircases at each end. The basement of The Briars once served as slave quarters.

Historically, The Briars is one of Natchez's most important homes because it was the girlhood home of Varina Howell, who became the wife of Jefferson Davis, the only president of the Confederate States of America. William Burr Howell, Varina's father and a relative of Aaron Burr, settled in Natchez after military service in the War of 1812. He married Louisa Kempe of the Virginia Kempes. The Howell family remained in The Briars until 1850.

Varina Howell's marriage to Jefferson Davis took place in the front parlor of The Briars on February 26, 1845. (The Confederate president had been married previously to Sarah Taylor, daughter of President Zachary Taylor. This first marriage was short-lived as Davis's bride died just months after the marriage.)

During the Civil War, the Walter Irvine family occupied The Briars. According to one historian, a shell from a Federal gunboat struck the house, tearing away one of the front gallery posts. After the war, the house slowly deteriorated until Mr. and Mrs. William Winnans Wall rescued it in 1927. The Walls restored The Briars to its original grandeur by furnishing it with items typical of the 1840s. The parklike grounds and beautifully restored house are open as a bed-and-breakfast inn.

# The Burn

John P. Walworth built The Burn in the 1830s and named his home after a small stream that once flowed near the house. Mr. Walworth had settled in Natchez after traveling down the Mississippi by steamboat from Ohio. Reportedly, his original destination was New Orleans, but Natchez enchanted him so that he decided to seek his fortune there instead. Walworth, who became a successful planter, merchant, and city mayor, contracted with the firm of Montgomery and Keyes to build his house, one of the oldest Greek Revival houses in the Natchez area. Descendants of the Walworth family occupied The Burn for almost one hundred years.

Ironically, The Burn, whose Scottish name means "the brook," did actually burn after it was built, resulting in a change of roof line, which altered the building from its original two-storied configuration to a rebuilt story-and-a-half format. A large ground-level area not visible from the front makes The Burn a two-and-a-half-story building in the rear. Thus, the interior of the house is much more spacious than its exterior in the front suggests. Also at the rear is a two-story brick building, which formerly served partly for family living quarters and partly as a garcionniere, or living space for the single young men and guests of the home.

Four fluted Doric columns support the wide, one-story front gallery of The Burn. The heavy, paneled door, framed with overhead and sidelights of rectangular hand-blown glass, opens to a large central hall whose most impressive feature is the curved stairway along one side. The cleverly designed stairway seems to defy gravity as it reaches the second story by turning away from the supporting wall and then making a half-turn upward.

The Burn has a rear gallery that overlooks part of a magnificent garden of numerous varieties of camellias and azaleas. The grounds, now only about four acres, were considerably larger when Walworth built the house. Many squares of present-day Natchez were once part of the estate of The Burn.

During the Civil War, the Union used The Burn as a hospital for troops as well as headquarters for Major John P. Coleman. Visitors can still see a name etched about this time into one of the window panes in the living room. At the time of this writing, the house, open to the public year-round, is operated as one of Natchez's more charming bed-and-breakfast inns by Mayor and Mrs. Tony Byrne.

THE BURN — ENTRANCE HALL AND STAIRCASE

THE BURN — PARLOR

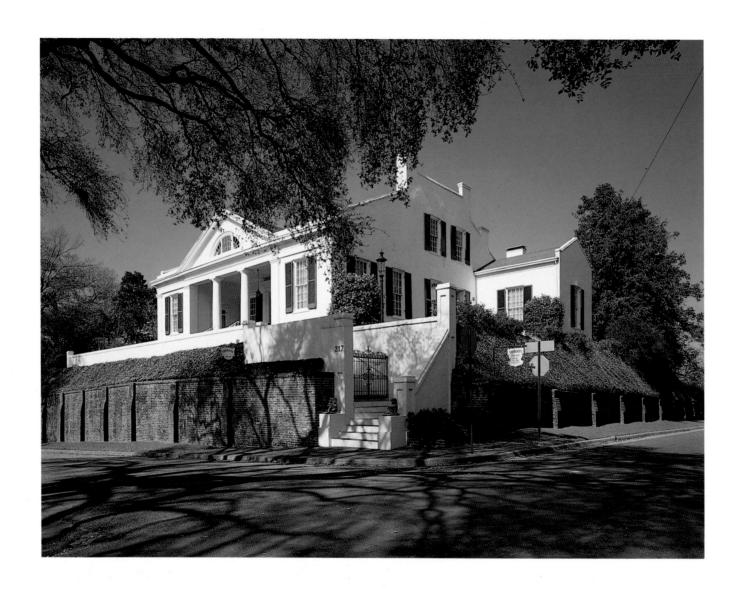

# Cherokee

Cherokee, an imposing, split-level home built in two stages, sits atop a hill near the center of old Natchez. Ebeneezer Rees acquired the property by grant from the Spanish government in April 1794; historians think that construction began a short time later. Architecturally, the original, rear section of the house shows obvious Spanish influence, primarily in its brick construction, which included brick flooring.

In 1810, the David Mishie family acquired the property. They later expanded and altered the house in the Greek Revival style. The most outstanding feature of this style at Cherokee is the recessed front gallery, which features two classic Doric columns at the front. An imposing entrance doorway opens to the central hall. A room stands on each side of the gallery: a formal parlor and a dining room. The central hallway opens at the rear to a spacious drawing room, which features a beautiful black marble fireplace flanked by two floor-to-ceiling windows overlooking an attractive rear garden.

Several small hallways off the drawing room open to bedroom areas, the kitchen, and a stairway. The brick stairway and retaining wall at the front of Cherokee feature attractive landscaping and a charming iron gate (a later addition) that opens to High Street.

Several of Cherokee's owners have figured in the history of Natchez. The controversial American military officer, Andrew Ellicott, sent to the city by the United States government to survey and set boundaries, had part of his encampment on the site. Because Natchez was still under Spanish rule, Ellicott's surveying for the Americans was hardly welcome. As a surveyor-general for the United States, Ellicott laid out many of the streets of Washington, D.C. Historians also credit him with the first accurate measurements of Niagara Falls.

From 1845 to 1858, wealthy and powerful Frederick Stanton lived at Cherokee. From here he watched the construction of his new and sumptuous home, Stanton Hall, built in the next block on High Street. It was completed in 1858.

George McPherson, a Natchez jeweler, lived in Cherokee during the Civil War period. After his tenure, a series of people owned the house and much deterioration took place. However, the Charles Byrne family rescued and restored the house. Mrs. Byrne was a descendant of the Metcalfe family, prominent residents of Natchez both historically and in the present day.

# D'Evereux

Occupying an almost perfect hillside setting, D'Evereux, one of Natchez's best examples of Greek Revival architecture, stands majestically against a background of oaks and magnolias.

Six fluted Doric columns, twelve feet apart and twenty-four feet tall, support a low, hipped roof topped at its peak by a cupola surrounded by a white balustrade. At D'Evereux's front, a small balcony featuring a delicate ironwork balustrade sits over the front entranceway, thus replacing the usual full second-floor gallery.

Another feature seldom seen in Natchez is a permanent two-step riser at the foot of the front stairs. Visitors used this riser, making entering and exiting carriages easier. The gallery at the rear extends across the house's entire width. The rear central entranceway features an elaborate curved fanlight over its door. The interior plan of D'Evereux consists of the "Natchez" central hallway flanked by four rooms: formal parlors on one side and dining room, stairway alcove, and service room on the opposite. The second floor repeats this layout, with two bedrooms on each side flanking the large central hallway.

Beyond the back of the house visitors can see three terraced gardens beautifully planted with varieties of camellias and azaleas. Beyond these gardens a lake, stocked with fish and adorned with white swans, once greeted guests. The restoration of the three gardens has been completed but not that of the lake.

William St. John Elliott built D'Evereux about 1840 and named it after his mother's family. In Natchez, Mr. Elliott gained his fortune as a planter. He married Anna Conner. The couple were leaders in Natchez society, entertaining often and lavishly at their beautiful estate. Henry Clay, noted statesman and close friend of the Elliotts, was entertained here in 1842. After the death of William Elliott in 1855, Anna Elliott closed the house and lived with her family at Cleremont, now called Belmont. During the Civil War, Federal troops camped on the property; they destroyed the gardens but spared the house. During this same period, the two murderers of John Sargent, master of nearby Gloucester, were hanged on the property. The murdered man was the last surviving son of Winthrop Sargent, once governor of the territory. Sometime after the Civil War, Mrs. Elliott returned to D'Evereux and lived there until her death in 1876. In 1925, D'Evereux was sold to Miss Myra Virginia Smith.

Miss Smith began a complete restoration. At her death she willed the house to her alma mater, the University of Chicago. It is now the home of Mrs. T. B. Buckles and the Jack Bensons, who graciously open the house and grounds to the public on a daily basis. The furnishings, many of them original to the house, are of museum quality.

# Dunleith

Built on one of Natchez's most imposing sites, Dunleith stands in templelike splendor. It was built about 1850 on the same spot that its owners' previous house, Routhland, stood. Routhland had been destroyed by a fire caused by lightning striking its tall chimneys.

Standing on pedestals, twenty-four tall Doric columns surround the house and support wide, double galleries, which feature railings of delicate ironwork on each level. Pedimented dormers project from the low, hipped roof: two each in the front and rear and one each on the sides. Four chimneys also symmetrically project from the roof. A two-story kitchen wing attaches at the house's rear. Dunleith's majestic presence is enhanced by its parklike surroundings. Visitors enter and exit its large, curved driveway through elaborate iron gates fronting Homochitto Street. Three Gothic outbuildings, dating from the original house, remain on the estate: a hothouse on the left and a stable and carriage house at the rear. The interior of Dunleith is just as magnificent. The large center hall and the square rooms on each side have been restored to old-world splendor. Marble fireplaces, beautiful chandeliers, drapes, carpets, and furnishings make the house a true Natchez showplace.

The house was built by Charles G. Dahlgren, the second husband of Mary Routh, whose father, Job Routh had amassed a large fortune from a land grant given to him by the Spanish.

Routh's gift to each of his children was a parcel of this land. Mr. Dahlgren was the son of Sweden's first U.S. consul and, reportedly, a descendant of King Gustavus Adolphus of Sweden. He came to Natchez after serving in the U.S. Navy and prospered as a banker. In his youth, Dahlgren had a reputation for a quick temper and is said to have had many scars proving his prowess as a dueler. Mary Dahlgren bore Charles seven children, all boys. Sarah Ann, Mary's daughter from her first marriage, is said to have been Charles's favorite. She was educated in many subjects not usually taught to women of that time and, as an adult, she became a prolific author.

During the Civil War, Sarah Ann worked both as a nurse and as a writer. After the war, she invited Jefferson Davis to her Gulf Coast summer home, Beauvoir, to live out his retirement. Here he wrote *The Rise and Fall of the Confederate Government.* Ironically, Charles Dahlgren, though a Confederate general in the Civil War, totally disagreed with Jefferson Davis's conduct of the war. The actions of his favorite stepdaughter upset him so much that he attempted to break her will, which left Beauvoir to the Confederate president.

Dunleith changed hands several times; its most consistent ownership lasted through several generations of the Carpenter family. It is presently the home of the W. F. Heins family and is open to the public on a regular basis.

# *Edgewood*

Mr. and Mrs. Samuel Hopkins Lambdin built Edgewood in 1859 on part of a land grant that the Spanish had awarded to John Bisland, Mrs. Lambdin's grandfather. The house was located on the edge of the heavily wooded Mount Repose estate, Mrs. Lambdin's home before her marriage. Thus, she and her husband called it Edgewood. The New Orleans architectural firm of Howard and Diettel designed the house. They were also the architects for Nottoway, Louisiana's largest plantation house located on the west bank of the Mississippi, just below Baton Rouge. Edgewood's builder was Thomas Rose of Natchez, who also built Stanton Hall.

The focal point of the house's facade is an arched French window in the center of the second floor. The break in the roof over this window gives emphasis to it. Elaborate brackets support the wide roof eaves. A portico, projecting across the front of the house, features eight fluted columns with Corinthian capitals. The brickwork for the chimney is sculpted rather than plain. Edgewood's exterior finish is a salmon-pink stucco.

Eight rooms, divided by central hallways on the two main levels, make up the basic floor plan. The main staircase is at the rear of the central hallway and is its focal point. Since the Lambdins built Edgewood on a hill, the rear of the house contains a third or basement level and the kitchen. The house includes a dumb waiter from the kitchen to the dining room, speaking tubes for communication to the service rooms, and water piped to some of the rooms from a storage tank—all unusual luxuries for the mid-nineteenth century.

James Reid Lambdin, a noted portrait painter and brother of Samuel Lambdin, is said to have painted some of his finest works while staying at Edgewood. The house, still elegant in its setting and filled with beautiful antiques, is home to Mr. Richard A. Campbell. Edgewood is shown to the public only during the spring Pilgrimage.

# *Elgin*

Elgin was built on property that was originally a land grant to Carlos White in 1791. At some later date Archibald Dunbar acquired the property but then lost it to the bank. Dr. John Jenkins purchased Elgin in 1839 for his bride, Annis Dunbar, the granddaughter of the Sir William Dunbar who served as the official surveyor of the Natchez Province. Originally from Scotland, Dunbar chose to remain in Natchez rather than return to his native land, even though family deaths would have allowed him to lead a titled lifestyle.

Elgin, built in stages, began as a building with low ceilings, which reflected the Spanish influence on its design. In 1840, Dr. Jenkins constructed a two-story addition to the original house. The addition features huge Doric columns supporting galleries at both levels. In 1853, Dr. Jenkins added a two-story brick building at the rear of the main house.

Originally from Pennsylvania, Dr. Jenkins decided to practice his profession in the Natchez area. Successful as a physician, he became even more noted for his horticultural endeavors. Jenkins studied every phase of the growing process and experimented with crop rotation, fertilization, and tree grafting to create different varieties of fruits and nuts. As a result of his training, he always recorded his findings in the scientific way. His experiments with packing fruit in ice to keep it fresh on its journey to the North were successful and ahead of their time. Interestingly, his methods are still used today.

In 1855, Dr. and Mrs. Jenkins became victims of yellow fever, dying a short time apart. However, their four children and their descendants remained at Elgin until 1914. The estate is presently the home of Dr. and Mrs. William F. Calhoun.

The architectural features of Elgin are somewhat basic since it is a typical, early Natchez plantation house. Rows of slender columns on each level support the double galleries across the ninety-foot front. To provide maximum ventilation, jib windows (windows set above small double doors) allow air to freely access the rooms of the house at both levels.

Inside, at the left of the house's central hall, is a large double parlor, which features floor-to-ceiling double doors alongside a large black marble fireplace. To the right of the hallway stands a high-ceilinged library with its own black marble fireplace. At the end of the hall, the dining room, obviously part of the earlier structure because of the much lower ceiling, has a hand-hewn punkah fan over the dining table.

Beautifully furnished, Elgin is open during the spring pilgrimage and currently accepts guests on a bed-and-breakfast basis.

# The Elms

The Elms is situated near downtown Natchez on South Pine Street at Washington. Its architecture, a somewhat eclectic blend of styles, results from its being built in three stages over a fifty-year period.

The original structure, completed in 1804, was a two-and-a-half-story dwelling with two rooms on each level. Low ceilings, thick walls, narrow windows, large chimneys, and heavy, handmade iron hinges suggest Spanish origins for this part of the house. John Henderson, who wrote the first book printed in Natchez, was an early owner. Louis Evans, the first American sheriff of Adams County, where Natchez is the seat of government, was another early owner. During the 1820s and 1830s, Rev. and Mrs. George Potts occupied the house, which served as the Presbyterian minister's residence.

In the years before the Civil War, The Elms became the residence of the David Stanton family. (He was a brother of Frederick Stanton, builder of Stanton Hall.) In 1856, David Stanton built the two-story frame addition, which enclosed a section of the original front gallery. Hallways in this gallery connected the older section to the new two-story frame. The new section consisted of a parlor on the first level and bedroom areas on the second. The Stantons also built a billiard hall in the side yard in the Greek Revival style.

Yet another owner, Moseley J. P. Drake, purchased the house in 1878 after renting it for a number of years. (He was the nephew of Benjamin M. Drake, a noted Methodist minister who had come to the Natchez area in 1824.) Succeeding interrelated generations of the Drake/Kellogg/Carpenter family have owned The Elms ever since. It is presently the home of Alma Carpenter. Now, the original one-hundred-acres-plus estate of The Elms has been reduced to about three acres, and most of the lost acreage is now downtown Natchez. Huge shrubs as well as elm and oak trees enhance the surroundings of the house.

The Elms contains a wrought-iron circular stairway, a one-of-a-kind in Natchez that may have come from Portugal. This stairway, part of the original gallery before it was enclosed during the 1856 remodeling, is the focal point of the entrance foyer. A system of calling bells still exists, each with a different tone, which, when rung in the servants' quarters, indicated to them which room to service.

Three brick cisterns supplied water to the house. The inhabitants of The Elms used one cistern for drinking and the others for washing and cooking. Three small octagon-shaped buildings also once stood on the grounds near the house. Though two have been destroyed, one still remains. Supposedly once housing a captive eagle, this building is now known as the Eagle House.

# Elms Court

One of the few houses in the Natchez area with the look of a Mediterranean villa, Elms Court stands distinctively white in its green, wooded, landscaped, suburban setting. The two-story central section of this house, built in 1836 by the Evans family, began as an almost-square Italian Renaissance villa. When the Turner family purchased the house in 1841, it was on record as being "Elms Court." Its next owner was millionaire Frank Surget, who purchased the house as a wedding present for his daughter Jane and her new husband, Ayres P. Merrill, in the late 1840s.

During this period of ownership, an architectural metamorphosis took place. The Merrills added one-story wings on each side; removed the original pillars from the gallery; and replaced these pillars with imported, delicate, grape-design, wrought-iron work, which extended across the front of the new sections. During this remodeling, the Merrills embellished the interior with fireplaces and intricate bronze chandeliers.

Although a southern aristocrat by birth, Mr. Merrill firmly believed in the Union. Immediately before the Civil War, he moved his family to the North. Mrs. Merrill died there without ever returning to her beloved Elms Court. In 1876, President Ulysses S. Grant, a close friend of Mr. Merrill, appointed him the United States ambassador to Belgium.

Elms Court has remained in the Surget family (Mrs. Merrill's family) throughout the years. It became a wedding present again when James Surget presented it to his daughter Carlotta at her marriage to David Lawrence McKittrick in 1895.

The McKittricks gave lavish parties, decorating the house beautifully and lighting it with candled chandeliers. An annual soiree given here during the early days of the Natchez Pilgrimage was called "The Ball of a Thousand Candles."

Some of the more notable guests at Elms Court throughout the years included Andrew Jackson, Jenny Lind, Lafayette, and William Makepeace Thackeray.

Presently Elms Court is the home of Mrs. Douglas H. MacNeil, daughter of Mr. and Mrs. David McKittrick. The house contains a collection of unusual decorations, including a carved punkah fan, originally covered in painted canvas.

Double parlors, a smoking room, and a billiard room flank one side of the long, central hallway of Elms Court. On the other side are a music room, library, and large banquet hall. The bedrooms are all on the second floor. Also of interest to today's visitors are the formal terraced gardens and the remains of a pit, which was once part of a gas manufacturing operation that produced fuel for lighting the house.

# Evans-Bontura

Because many people have owned this house, it has been called Evansview, The Market House, Bontura, and the Smith-Bontura-Evans House. Resembling a New Orleans or a Mobile town house more than a Natchez home, Evans-Bontura stands high on the bluffs in Natchez on Broadway Street, with a grand view of the Mississippi. Just across the street is the entrance to "Natchez Under-the-Hill."

The building, as it stands, was constructed in several stages. The first, rear section was constructed about 1790, during the Spanish regime. This two-story, one-room-deep structure has wide balconies on the second level. Arched openings on the ground floor formerly served as entrances to stables for the carriages of the commercial taxi business that Robert Smith, a free man of color, operated in Natchez in the 1850s.

Most historians credit Mr. Smith with building the front town-house section in the early 1850s. This part of the house consists of a small entry hall to the left, opening to a parlor to its right with a wide room behind, which spans the width of the house. Fireplaces stand at each end of this large room, which also has a large window opening to the courtyard at the left and a rear door opening to a gallery.

This gallery was part of an 1860 addition that connected the original building to the town-house section. The second floor contains two bedrooms. One can reach a third-level attic space, lighted by a centered single dormer, by a small stairway.

The double front galleries, with their lacy cast-iron grillwork, were added in the 1890s.

Mr. Joseph Bontura acquired the house in 1853. An immigrant from Portugal and the owner of a successful business in "Natchez Under-the-Hill," Mr. Bontura bought the Smith property for use as an inn. The house suffered some damage during the Civil War from shelling by a Federal gunboat, the USS *Essex*. Some of the more notable figures entertained at the house were Stephen Foster, Mark Twain, and Captain Tom Leathers, whose steamboat *Natchez* was made famous by its historical race with the *Robert E. Lee*.

In 1941, Mr. and Mrs. Tom Evans of Los Angeles acquired the house. They restored and furnished it beautifully and later donated it to the Mississippi Chapter of Colonial Dames, who presently operate it as a museum house. It is opened to the public during the spring Pilgrimage.

# Fair Oaks

Built about 1822 in what was then known as the fashionable Second Creek Neighborhood, Fair Oaks is a ninety-eight-foot-wide, low, planter-type house. Henry W. Huntington, who had married Helen Dunbar, the daughter of Sir William Dunbar of nearby Forest Plantation, constructed the house in 1822 and named it Green Oak.

In 1836, John Hutchins acquired the property and changed its name to Woodbourn. Twenty years later, in 1856, Dr. Orrick Metcalfe, a graduate of the Yale School of Medicine, bought the estate. He changed the name of his home to Fair Oaks. The property has remained in the Metcalfe family ever since.

The original building, only one room deep, was constructed of hand-hewn cypress joined with wooden pegs. The ninety-eight-foot gallery, obviously designed to be utilized as part of the living space, includes finely detailed, paneled wainscoting, chair rails, and jib-doors under the six windows. These allow access to and ventilation of all the rooms that open to the gallery, which is surrounded by a wooden railing. Eight slender columns support the gallery roof, which is part of the main roof.

Visitors enter a room-sized entrance hall through a fan- and side-lighted Federal doorway. (The doorway design is similar to that of Hawthorne.) An unusual feature of the large entrance hall is its fireplace. The entrance to the dining room, an early addition, repeats the lights of the hall. The predominant feature of the beautifully furnished dining room is a naturally finished punkah fan, which resembles a hoop-skirted lady.

Mr. and Mrs. Bazile R. Lanneau own Fair Oaks and open it for tours during the spring Pilgrimage. Mr. Lanneau is the great-grandson of Dr. Metcalfe.

# Glenburnie

Natchez attorney Sturges Sprague and his wife, Frances, built this single-story Mississippi planter's cottage on property that Mrs. Sprague had acquired about 1833. The grounds were originally part of a Spanish land grant awarded to Adam Bingaman in the late 1790s. The Federal-style house features a wide gallery recessed under the gable roof. Slender Doric columns, with a wooden balustrade between them, support the gallery. Visitors enter a small, center hallway through a fanlighted classic doorway. H. G. Bulkly, the owner of the house in 1901, built an addition that included an extension of the wide gallery. For some reason, however, this addition did not match the spindled balustrade, and the result appears to be simply an addition and not an integral part of the house.

The house attracted national attention in 1932 when Miss Jennie Merrill, then residing there, was brutally murdered. Miss Merrill, a descendant of the prominent Surget and Dunbar families, was born in 1864 at nearby Elms Court. After the death of Mr. Merrill in 1890, the beautiful and educated Jennie sold the property, and eventually bought Glenburnie in 1904.

As Miss Jennie grew older, she became eccentric, antisocial, and conservative. The only person with whom she associated was Duncan G. Minor, her second cousin. For thirty years Mr. Minor called on the reclusive lady, always visiting her by horseback from his house, Oakland. Gossip abounded about the pair. Some stories said they were in love since childhood but unable to marry because of family feuds and threats of disinheritance. Other tales insisted that the two were secretly married.

In the summer of 1932, when Jennie was sixty-eight years old, Mr. Minor reported to the local sheriff that she was missing. When the police found her body, their chief suspects were an eccentric couple who lived next door. Richard "Dick" Dana and Octavia Dockery lived in complete squalor in Glenwood, a once-resplendent mansion, allowing goats, cows, and pigs the run of the house.

Miss Jennie had attempted to get her neighbors to control their animals, resulting in several acrimonious lawsuits. The sheriff naturally suspected Dockery and Dana of murdering her. However, the courts convicted the robber George Pearls of the crime. Still, the pair and their house, Glenwood (now known as Goat Castle), became famous. They opened their home as a tourist attraction; but after the death of Miss Dockery, Glenwood fell into complete disrepair and developers soon tore it down.

Glenburnie, however, remains a beautifully restored mansion. Its owners, Mr. and Mrs. George Guide, show the house during the fall Pilgrimage.

# Gloucester

About 1800, Samuel Young built Gloucester, which is readily recognizable by its Federal detailed front portico. When Winthrop Sargent purchased the home in 1807, he named it after his home town of Gloucester, Massachusetts. President John Adams had appointed Mr. Sargent to be the first governor of the Mississippi Territory.

The facade of Gloucester, a red-brick structure, features a giant Grecian portico supported by four massive Tuscan columns. The entrance is quite unusual: Gloucester has two separate, slightly recessed, entrance doors, identically designed with semicircular fanlights above. These doors stand at each end of the portico. Side-lights alongside the dual entrance doors are also unusual in that they serve as separate narrow windows alongside the doorway trim.

A dry moat surrounds the house's basement level, which once contained service rooms. Each end of the one-room-deep house is shaped as one-half of an octagon. The hipped roof at the rear of the building covers a recessed gallery at both levels. Closed service rooms stand at each end of these galleries. Dependency buildings at the side of the house include the original kitchen, a cistern, and a billiard room with bedrooms above.

The dual entrance doors (which confused first-time visitors who didn't know which one to enter) open to a U-shaped hallway, which runs the width of the portico and extends down the length of the house on both sides. These two side hallways feature mahogany-trimmed stairways. The plan of the first floor consists of a formal drawing room on the right, a large dining room at the left, and a library between the two stairway halls. Upstairs are three large bedrooms.

Gloucester has always been elaborately furnished, and its beautiful marble mantels and crystal chandeliers remain intact. The furniture, paintings, mirrors, and other accessories are of museum quality.

Interestingly, Gloucester was sold after the death of Winthrop Sargent, but George Washington Sargent, his son, repurchased it twenty-five years later. Reportedly, during the Union occupation, marauding Yankee soldiers killed George Sargent at the back door of the house. He is buried in the Gloucester cemetery. (Winthrop Sargent died and was buried at sea in 1820. The family placed a marker in the Gloucester cemetery in his memory.)

Though at the time of this writing visitors could not tour Gloucester, the owners plan to open the house for tours upon completion of the ongoing renovation. This home is one of the oldest and most significant in the Natchez area.

# Green Leaves

Built in two stages, Green Leaves took shape, sometime before the War of 1812, as a town house for Jonathan Thompson. His family became victims of yellow fever in 1820. Reportedly, all of them, including Mr. Thompson, died within a week. In 1849, George Washington Koontz acquired the house, which had been lived in by several owners after the Thompsons' deaths. A transplant from Pennsylvania, Mr. Koontz later became a partner in the firm of Britton and Koontz, a bank that played a part in Natchez history and still exists today. Mr. Koontz expanded Green Leaves to its present form.

President Jefferson Davis sent Mr. Koontz to Europe during the Civil War to seek and negotiate loans for the Confederacy. Because of his close affiliation with bankers and his part in the South's war effort, Koontz was unpopular during the days of Reconstruction.

The classic architectural style of Green Leaves features a brick-and-frame construction and a hipped roof with a glass-enclosed cupola at its peak. Wrought-iron trim adorns the front galleries of the side-wing additions. A small front entrance gallery features two fluted Doric columns; the elaborate entrance doorway, with side-lights on each side and a rectangular fanlight overhead, is almost as wide as this gallery. Visitors can still see a bullet hole in the overhead glass—the result of an assassination attempt on the life of Mr. Koontz during Reconstruction days.

The back of Green Leaves and the galleries flanking the two rear wings enclose a beautifully planted courtyard, which a huge oak, said to be almost four hundred years old, dramatically shades. Because the Natchez Indians supposedly once held council meetings beneath this ancient oak, past owners of Green Leaves called it Council Oak.

One of Mr. Koontz's daughters married Melchoir S. Beltzhoover, a member of another prominent Natchez family. Descendants of the Koontz/Beltzhoover families have made Green Leaves their home ever since.

Most of Green Leaves' original furnishings remain. Visitors to this historic house can view beautifully carved redwood furniture, large gold-leafed mirrors, black marble fireplace mantles, and personal items (including correspondence between President Davis and Mr. Koontz).

GREEN LEAVES — PARLOR

GREEN LEAVES — GAME ROOM

GREEN LEAVES — DINING ROOM

# *Hawthorne*

The smallish-appearing exterior of this typical, early Southern, plantation-style house belies a commodious interior. Hawthorne was built about 1814 as a story-and-a-half cottage featuring a Federal detailed double entrance door complete with attractive fan- and side-lights, all with hand-blown glass panes. The two doorways in Hawthorne's central hall and the door at the rear of the hall repeat these fanlights. This hall opens to the parlor on one side and to the dining room on the other. The interior ceilings are high, and the rooms are large. Fireplaces in the Federal style grace both the parlor and dining room.

An arch with Doric columns at the base on each side separates the front and back of the large central hallway. The front section is smaller than the rear, which contains a stairway to the attic floor. The front gallery, extending the width of the house, was probably added in the mid-1880s. The construction of the walls is brick-between-heavy-wooden-beams. All the exterior walls, except the front wall along the gallery, are coated with clapboard. Stucco covers the front wall.

Historians credit Jonathan Thompson with the construction of Hawthorne. Thompson, a real estate developer, married the stepdaughter of Winthrop Sargent, Mississippi's first territorial governor. Reportedly, the Thompsons became victims of yellow fever, both dying several years after building their home. Other notable families who have owned Hawthorne were the Overakers and the Dunbars. Lafayette is said to have been entertained here in 1825.

Presently Hawthorne (assumed to have been named after the Hawthorn shrub, which abounds in the area) is the property of Mr. and Mrs. Hyde Dunbar Jenkins, who show their beautifully furnished home to the public during the spring Pilgrimage.

# Hope Farm

One of the few houses remaining in Natchez from the colonial period, Hope Farm is a quaint, simple structure, built in two stages and located on Homochitto Street. Marcus Hailer constructed the first, or rear, wing in 1775, during the British regime. Several years later, Don Carlos de Grand Pre, the Spanish governor of the territory, acquired the property. Utilizing Spanish Provincial architectural stylings, Don Carlos added a new section to the house in 1789.

Features of the new construction include the use of wooden pegs and tongue-in-groove to connect the cypress structural beams; wide overhanging eaves; and the use of stucco on the front wall, which opens to a deep gallery. The low roof is hipped on one end and gabled at the other. Don Carlos added his new wing at a right angle to the original structure and planted gracious gardens in the L-shape, which the addition created.

In 1805, George Overaker, the owner and operator of The White Horse Tavern, also located on Homochitto Street, bought the property. The Montgomery family acquired it in 1835. Hope Farm remained in that family for over ninety years—until 1926. At that time, Mr. and Mrs. J. Balfour Miller bought the house and began an immediate and accurate restoration of the estate. A prominent couple in Natchez social circles, the Millers furnished Hope Farm with family heirlooms from their own colonial heritage.

Besides the interesting and functional furnishings, visitors can see many unusual artifacts: a cleverly designed "punishing chair," used by early schoolmasters to discipline wayward students, and a wooden figurehead from a Mississippi River steamboat named *Natchez*. (To date, seven steamboats have carried that name. The *SS Natchez VII* still plies the river as a tourist excursion boat in New Orleans.) Natchezians credit Mrs. J. Balfour Miller with being the driving force behind the concept of the Natchez Pilgrimage in 1932.

Hope Farm is presently the home of Mrs. Ethel Green and her family. The house, featured on the spring Pilgrimage tour, is open year-round for bed-and-breakfast guests.

# The House on Ellicott's Hill

The United States government sent Andrew Ellicott, a major in the army, to survey and set boundaries in the Natchez area. He set his camp on the hill on which this structure, also known as Connelly's Tavern, was built. Historians credit Major Ellicott, who raised the American flag on the site in 1797, with being the first to do so in the lower Mississippi Valley.

James Moore, a Natchez merchant, built The House on Ellicott's Hill around 1798. He purchased the land from the mother-in-law of Manuel Gayoso de Lemos, the Spanish governor. Samuel Brooks, the first mayor of Natchez, once resided at the house. Later, Dr. Frederick Seip, one of the first physicians in the Natchez Territory, lived there.

Professor E. J. Cornish operated The House on Ellicott's Hill as the Natchez High School for Boys. After the Civil War, Professor W. Gilreath owned and operated the school until difficulties forced its closing in 1878. Still later, this mansion housed cotton mill employees until the mills closed.

Part brick and part wood, The House on Ellicott's Hill is West Indies/Spanish Provincial in style. During the years in which the house was used as a tavern, the first floor, with its brick floors, low ceilings, and rather spartan details, served as the tap room and kitchen. The second floor, with French windows, ornamental moldings, carved mantels, and more sophisticated detailing, housed guests.

Much of the material the builder used in constructing the two stories of The House on Ellicott's Hill came from dismantled flatboats and shipping vessels. A gallery with wooden rails and slender columns extends across the wide front of both stories. These galleries provide a commanding view of the Mississippi. The attractive canted roof is both hipped and gabled. The parlor of the house features a rather unusual architectural feature—a deep decorative dome in the center of the plastered ceiling, apparently designed to trap the smoke from the candle- or oil-lit ceiling fixture.

The House on Ellicott's Hill was the first restoration project of the Natchez Garden Club, which insisted on completing its work with authentic furnishings that accorded with the 1819 estate inventory of Dr. Seip. This authenticity makes The House on Ellicott's Hill most interesting. The house is open to visitors throughout the year and both the spring and the fall Pilgrimage feature it.

# Lansdowne

This suburban mansion, an attractive blend of beautifully preserved Georgian and Greek Revival architecture, stands in a parklike setting a mile or so from downtown Natchez, off Pine Ridge Road. Mr. and Mrs. George Marshall built Lansdowne in 1853. Mrs. Marshall was the daughter of David Hunt, one of the wealthiest men in the Mississippi Valley. A true cotton king, her father owned more than twenty plantations in Mississippi and Louisiana. His wedding present to his daughter originally consisted of a six-hundred-acre-plus tract. Another gift shortly after increased the extensive estate.

On their property, the Marshalls built a one-story house with a lower basement and a white-railed captain's walk, also called a widow's walk or belvedere, at the peak of the roof. (They intended ultimately to add a second story, but today the structure remains as it was originally built.) Each of the six chimneys has two flues. A smallish front portico with a pedimented roof features four fluted columns; wrought-iron railings; and a wide, curving, entrance stairway.

The modest appearance of Lansdowne's exterior is deceiving. Though it appears to be a small building, the interior proportions are quite massive, as the central hall measures fifteen feet by sixty-five feet. A stairway, entered from the pantry, leads to a finished attic room lighted by a band of ten windows, which frame the captain's walk above. Formal rooms stand on one side of the hallway and bedrooms on the other.

At the rear of the house, a gallery opens to a bricked courtyard flanked by two-story service buildings. The buildings housed a billiard room, commissary, school room, the governess's room, and a gas plant. (The manufacturing of gas on-site was quite an oddity for its time as most southern towns had not yet acquired such systems.)

Accustomed to the "good life," George Marshall, son of a wealthy banker, spent much of his time traveling, acquiring possessions, and improving his estate. The furnishings at Lansdowne, original to the house, prove the taste and interests of the Marshalls. Aubusson carpets, hand-blocked Zuber and Delicourt wallpaper, white fireplace mantles, silver-plated door knobs, elaborate bronze chandeliers, impressive classic furniture, oil paintings, art objects, and Old Paris china make Lansdowne a true house-museum.

The Civil War brought near disaster to the estate when Union soldiers, raiding houses in the area, approached Lansdowne, stalked into the house, and confronted Mrs. Marshall. She stood her ground, but one of the marauders struck her in the face; a scar from this encounter remained with her until her death.

Fortunately the soldiers did not destroy the house; however, they did steal the Marshalls' famous collection of apricot-trimmed china, breaking and strewing it along the road as they left. Reportedly, George Marshall was at Lansdowne at the time of the raid, recovering from wounds he had received at the 1862 Battle of Shiloh, where he served as a colonel in the Confederate army.

Lansdowne has remained in the Marshall family throughout the years. It is presently the home of the George M. Marshall family and has the distinction of never having gone through a restoration; its owners have carefully preserved it. The family cemetery, on the grounds, is still in use. George M. Marshall I, II, and III are buried there. Lansdowne is open to the public.

LANSDOWNE — PARLOR

# Linden

No one seems to know exactly when James Moore, a Natchez merchant, built Linden. However, because of the type of construction and the materials used, historians generally agree that builders for Mr. Moore completed the center, two-storied section between 1785 and 1792.

Records show that Thomas Reed, one of the first U.S. senators from Mississippi, acquired the property in 1818. Most historians credit Senator Reed with the addition of the wings on each side of the original structure, the long gallery extending ninety-eight feet across the front of the house, and a second-story portico over the center of the long gallery. Ten Doric columns support the roof of the gallery, which has a balustrade atop its entire length.

Historians also credit Senator Reed with the handsome front-entrance doorway with its exquisite fanlight above; its side-lights, shaped in a diamond and oval pattern, on each side; and its flanking Grecian pilasters. (The movie *Gone with the Wind* made Linden's doorway famous by copying its design for Tara.) After the death of Senator Reed, Dr. John Ker, the senator's close friend and associate, acquired the estate. He named it Linden and probably added the present dining room to the house. (Dr. Ker gained notoriety for his involvement in a legal battle concerning the slaves of Captain Isaac Ross, father of the widow of Senator Reed. In his will, Captain Ross requested that his slaves be set free after his death. At the time, Mississippi law directly forbade such a proposal.)

Sometime in 1849, Mrs. Jane (Gustine) Conner, widow of William C. Conner, bought Linden. To create more living area and service rooms, Mrs. Conner built the west wing behind the house. The combination of additions created an attractive courtyard setting. Because seven of Mrs. Conner's sons served in the Confederate army, the South dubbed her the "little war mother." Her descendants still live at Linden.

The house contains a treasury of outstanding Federal furnishings; an impressive white cypress, painted, punkah fan; several first-edition Audubon prints; and a multitude of interesting accent pieces and artifacts of historical interest. The bedrooms in the additions built by Mr. Reed and Mrs. Conner presently serve as accommodations for overnight guests in this most attractive Natchez home. Linden is currently the residence of the Richard Conner Feltus family, who graciously show the house daily to visitors and to overnight guests on a bed-and-breakfast basis.

# Longwood

Longwood, the largest and most elaborately planned octagonal house in America, stands incomplete as a symbol and reminder of the effect of the American Civil War on the lifestyle of the South's affluent planter class.

Dr. and Mrs. Haller Nutt began to build Longwood as a home for themselves and their eight children in 1860. Dr. Nutt was a doctor, scientist, landowner, and planter. His father, Dr. Rush Nutt, was known internationally for his improvements in cottonseed variety and in the machinery planters used to process the cotton.

As his architect, Dr. Nutt selected Samuel Sloan from Philadelphia, who had published plans and specifications for an octagonal house in his book, *Model Architect.* Actual construction of the huge thirty-two room mansion progressed at a rather rapid pace. Mr. Sloan, brought most of the artisans and construction workers, who were specialists, from Philadelphia.

The eight-sided brick building, which is six stories high, features a central rotunda, open for five of the floors. Rooms encircle this rotunda on each level. These rooms open either to a verandah or to a balcony. One steps onto the balconies through large floor-to-ceiling openings. The balconies feature pillars with elaborately carved capitals and bases. The tall, wide, arched windows, which open to the verandahs, were designed to have sliding shutters that would be concealed in the hollow of the wall alongside. Unfortunately, this unique future was never completed.

The center rotunda at the lower levels was to be lighted by large mirrors reflecting sunlight from the sixteen windows of the upper-level observatory, but again the Civil War halted these plans. The sixteen windows were situated to provide cross-ventilation to help cool the lower floors. In addition, the house is topped by an onion-shaped "oriental" dome.

Appointments for Longwood were to include a splendid circular stairway for the multi-floored rotunda, marble mantles, statues for the multitude of niches built into the interior walls, mosaic flooring, and specially designed furniture to match the eight-sided structure's interior walls. Because these costly accouterments were enroute to Natchez when the Civil War began, officials of the Union blockade confiscated many of them.

By the fall of 1861, builders had completed the exterior of Longwood, with the exception of the installation of some windows and the outer stairs. Unfortunately for the owners, the announcement of the beginning of the American Civil War halted construction because the Philadelphia workers immediately deserted the construction site, leaving behind tools, equipment, and even open paint cans.

With the help of local artisans, Dr. Nutt managed to finish the basement of Longwood and then move his family into the house. However, his fortune disappeared when Federal troops burned or seized his cotton fields, worth millions of dollars. Broken and dejected, Dr. Nutt died in 1864.

Three generations of the Nutt family lived in the basement level of the unfinished mansion for more than a century. In 1968, the heirs sold the house and ninety acres of land to the Kelly McAdams Foundation of Texas, which later donated the estate to the Natchez Pilgrimage Garden Club. The house and grounds, still owned and operated by the club, are open daily for tours. Longwood has a National Historic Landmark designation. Because of its unfinished state (it remains almost as it was in 1864), visitors wondering about construction techniques and materials of that period find the house especially interesting.

LONGWOOD — DINING ROOM

LONGWOOD — BEDROOM

# Magnolia Hall

In 1858, builders completed Magnolia Hall as a residence for Mr. Thomas Henderson, a wealthy planter, merchant, and cotton broker. His father, John Henderson, had emigrated from Scotland to Natchez in 1787. The Henderson family home, Pleasant Hill, originally stood on the site, but the Hendersons moved it a short distance away to make room for this much more imposing structure.

In its bracketed cornice and arched panels in the entrance door, the architecture of Magnolia Hall reflects the influence of the then-popular Italianate style. The imposing projecting portico features four large fluted Ionic columns supporting a second-story gallery and a large, ornate, pedimented roof. The brick construction of the house is stuccoed and painted to resemble brown stones. Unlike most Natchez mansions, Magnolia Hall has an attached kitchen and servants' quarters. Magnolia blossoms dominate the design of the ceiling medallions in the parlor of the house, thus the derivation of its name.

This home was the last great mansion built in Natchez before the Civil War. Magnolia Hall suffered some damage from shelling by a Union gunboat in 1862. After the war, the Britton family, prominent Natchez merchants, owned Magnolia Hall. In the 1940s, Mr. and Mrs. George W. Armstrong purchased the house. During that period it operated as a boarding house called "Magnolia Inn." It also served for a while as an Episcopal day school. In 1970, Mrs. George Armstrong donated the property to the Natchez Garden Club, which has maintained it ever since as a continuing restoration project.

Visitors to Magnolia Hall, which houses a most interesting costume museum, can see furniture purchased by Mr. Henderson, the original owner, as well as other lovely pieces that match items listed in the inventory of his estate. Magnolia Hall is open daily for tours and is one of the properties featured in the spring and fall Pilgrimages.

MAGNOLIA HALL — LIBRARY

MAGNOLIA HALL — BEDROOM

MAGNOLIA HALL — PARLOR

# Melrose

Melrose stands almost exactly as it did in the 1840s—in a beautiful, parklike setting, complete with a circular drive and a picturesque pond embellished with some of Natchez's few cypress trees. Natchez attorney John T. McMurran and his wife Mary built the house. Mr. McMurran, originally from Pennsylvania, came to Natchez in the middle 1820s.

The Natchez architect and builder John Byers designed Melrose with a blending of Georgian and Greek Revival styles similar to Rosalie. The two-story, red-brick house features a rather large portico on its facade. Four large Doric columns support an iron-balustraded second-story balcony and a pedimented roof projection. An oversized widow's walk, or belvedere, the largest in Natchez, enhances the peak of the hipped roof. Across the front of the house, symmetrical windows and formal Greek doorways grace both floors. At the rear of the house, the first owners used two brick dependencies as a kitchen and slave quarters.

The spacious central hall divides into a front foyer section and, through a fanlighted and side-lighted doorway, into a larger rear hallway, which an 1865 inventory describes as a "saloon." The builders embellished the sliding doors of the double parlors with Ionic pilasters along their frames. A third room, the library, opens into the other two through a similar wide doorway. Thus, former owners could entertain in a three-room salon.

The left side of the lower floor consists of a large dining room, with an elaborate, carved, mahogany punkah fan hanging over the table. A stairway climbs along the side of the large central hallway. In back of the stairs, service rooms and the pantry complete the lower floor. Six bedrooms on the second floor stand alongside the center hallway. The verandah at the rear of both floors is as wide as the building.

Melrose's builder and first owner held on to the property throughout the Civil War. However, he had to sell the estate in 1865. Mr. McMurran's bad fortune continued as he lost his life about a year later in a steamboat accident near Baton Rouge. Heirs of Mr. George Marlin Davis, the Natchez attorney who bought the house from Mr. McMurran, lived in the house until 1976 when Mr. and Mrs. John S. Callon acquired it. In 1988, Melrose became the centerpiece of the newly established Natchez National Historic Park after the park service purchased it from the Callon estate.

Because of the relative continuity of ownership over the lifetime of Melrose, and the decision by its owners to refurbish rather than remodel, the house is said to have more original furnishings than most Natchez homes. Featured in this house are unique hand-painted floor cloths, marble fireplaces, and Cornelius brass lighting fixtures and chandeliers from Philadelphia, Pennsylvania. Melrose is open daily for tours and is also shown during the Pilgrimages.

MELROSE — REAR VIEW WITH AUXILIARY BUILDINGS

# Mistletoe

Although Mistletoe is the smallest house in this collection, it is unusual in its own way. John Bisland, who had come to Natchez sometime in the late 1700s, built the house in 1807. Through land grants from the Spanish government, he accumulated a large amount of land. Mistletoe was his wedding present to his son, Peter, and his son's bride, Barbara Foster.

Because he had been given a classical education by his generous father, Peter Bisland chose a lifestyle quite different from his more ambitious cotton-growing peers'. Appreciating the beauty of nature and the joy of learning, he remained a scholar until his accidental death in 1829. According to one obituary of record, he drowned in a cistern while seeking water to alleviate a fever, which had made him delirious.

The house, always a home, is a simple story-and-a-half planter's cottage, which has remained in the same family since it was first built. However, the interior of the upper floor, which one reaches through a staircase on the back porch, has never been finished. A wide gallery runs the entire width of the house at the front.

The original floor plan, before later additions, consisted of four rooms divided by a central hallway. The entry is through somewhat slender double doors spanned above by a half-circular fanlight. Side-lights on each side feature rectangular and square panes of glass, which shutters on the inside can cover. Unusually large symmetrical windows along the Palladian doorway open to a sitting room on the left and a bedroom on the right.

Cypress floors throughout Mistletoe and the sitting room walls paneled with cypress boards, finished in a natural state, are quite lovely. The trim, moldings (including those on the elaborate fireplace mantles), chair rails, and baseboards are all in the Federal style. The sitting room's large fireplace is not centered but placed closer to the rear wall. The architect probably designed it this way to help heat the smaller library room behind, which has no fireplace.

Additions to the house include a large room used for dining, built in the 1840s; a windowed gallery across the rear of the house; and kitchen and bedroom wings added in the twentieth century to make the house more functional for present-day living.

Because of the continuity of family ownership, the antique treasures and heirlooms accumulated throughout the years are as impressive as those seen in many of the more prestigious Natchez mansions. The house is usually open to visitors during the Pilgrimages.

# Monmouth

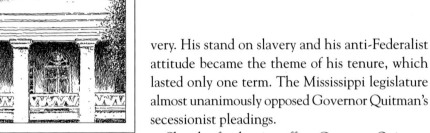

This large brick mansion was built in about 1818. The home was constructed for John Hankinson, once the postmaster of Natchez. A native of New Jersey, he named his estate after his birthplace — Monmouth County. The Hankinsons lived at Monmouth just a few short years before dying of yellow fever, which the couple contracted from a stranger they befriended.

The most famous owner of Monmouth was John Quitman, who acquired the property a short time after the death of the Hankinsons. Mr. Quitman, one of Mississippi's most notable early citizens, rose to fame and fortune first in state politics, then in the military, and finally in federal politics. His strong personality won him his first political victory over an established incumbent, who he defeated for a seat in the state legislature. His success as a representative in the legislature propelled him into the state Senate.

Next, Mr. Quitman became a general in the Mexican War, during which he victoriously raised the American flag over the Mexican capital, the first ever to do so. General Quitman returned home a military hero, and the citizens of Mississippi quickly elected him governor. Though born in the North, the son of a preacher, Governor Quitman became one of the earliest proponents of states' rights and adamantly supported slavery. His stand on slavery and his anti-Federalist attitude became the theme of his tenure, which lasted only one term. The Mississippi legislature almost unanimously opposed Governor Quitman's secessionist pleadings.

Shortly after leaving office, Governor Quitman became Congressman Quitman of the U.S. House of Representatives. During his time in Washington, he became involved in a failed attempt at a coup to overthrow the government of Cuba. Congressman Quitman's death came from poisoning at a banquet he attended to honor President Buchanan in 1858. Modern-day historians speculate that the congressman actually died from what is now known as "Legionnaire's Disease."

The house in which Mr. Quitman lived features a two-story portico and an unusually large pedimented roof. Four massive pillars support the portico and roof. A remarkable zig-zag–patterned balustrade on the second floor of the gallery complements the strong, masculine appearance of this house.

Monmouth is beautifully furnished with many pieces of its most notable period, that of the Quitmans. The house features attractive Adam-style, carved woodwork. In addition, *faux-bois* doors (doors of wood painted with a grain design) are prominent. Its long, curved stairway opens to the central hallway. Thus, the stairway differs somewhat from the usual Natchez stairway built off a side hall.

In 1978, Ron and Lani Riches restored Monmouth, one of Natchez's premier houses. They currently operate it as a nine-teen-room hotel, which is listed by *Country Inn* and *USA Today* as one of the finest small luxury hotels in the world. The public can view the house during the Pilgrimages.

MONMOUTH — GENERAL
QUITMAN BEDROOM

MONMOUTH — DINING ROOM

MONMOUTH — ENTRY HALL

# Montaigne

Builders completed Montaigne in 1855 for General William T. Martin, an aide to General Robert E. Lee and one of Mississippi's highest ranking Confederate generals. General Martin's features, carved on Stone Mountain near Atlanta, Georgia, represent the state of Mississippi in that monument to the Confederacy. The name *Montaigne* is the French Huguenot word for Martin.

General Martin, though a slave owner, disapproved of that institution and publicly advocated the resettlement of American slaves in Africa. Despite his beliefs, however, he remained loyal to the Confederacy and served that cause heroically in the Civil War. After the war, General Martin practiced law and became active in politics. Involved also in business, he served as president of the Natchez-Jackson-Columbus Railroad. He died in Natchez in 1910.

According to rumor, Union troops occupied Montaigne during the war. Supposedly, they used the front parlors as stables and the grand piano as a feedbox for the horses.

The house as it now stands is a story-and-a-half brick structure, stuccoed in pink. The peak of the hipped roof boasts a balustered widow's walk, or belvedere. A classic Greek entrance-portico features four slender white columns and a mosaic floor. Small galleries are attached to each side of the house. Montaigne's 1927 remodeling included many interior alterations, but the architects chose to keep the classic doorway surrounds and fireplace mantles.

The Kendall family has owned Montaigne for years. Family members who occupy the mansion at this time include the former Mrs. William J. Kendall, now Mrs. Hunter Goodrich. Mrs. Goodrich, a native of Natchez, had ancestors in the area before 1792. Montaigne, on the National Register of Historic Places, is open for tours only during the Pilgrimages. It is known for its gardens, which feature azaleas and several hundred varieties of camellias.

# Mount Repose

Mount Repose, an excellent example of an early Southern plantation house, is located on the outskirts of Natchez, on what was once Pine Ridge Road, but which has since been renamed Martin Luther King Road. William Bisland built the original, center section of the house in 1824 on land his father, John Bisland, acquired by grant from Spain in 1786.

Because its interior is much more spacious than is apparent from the outside, the size of Mount Repose is deceiving. The builders constructed the wood-frame house with hand-hewn timber and wooden pegs. The main portion of the house has two stories, with a double, front gallery (thought to have been added at a later date because of its roof angle), which features six square columns on each level and a wooden balustrade on the second level.

The house has one-story wings on each side, an enclosed stairway at its rear, and a central hallway on both levels. The entrance doorway features side-lights and a fanlight above. Because of its hexagon shape, the service building at the rear of Mount Repose is unique.

Because Mount Repose has remained in the same family since being built, its numerous authentic heirlooms and records are intact. These treasures include letters written to John Bisland by his sons while they attended school in Scotland. Judge W. B. Shields (a figure in the famous Aaron Burr trial for treason) once owned one of these heirlooms, a cherry desk made by a slave cabinet-maker.

Of the many interesting stories about Mount Repose, one repeatedly told is about William Bisland, who built the mansion. Mr. Bisland vowed that he would design a front entrance drive to his new home only if the voters elected Henry Clay, his close friend, to the presidency. Because Clay lost the election, visitors enter the grounds of Mount Repose from the side rather than the front!

During the Reconstruction period after the Civil War, Miss Elizabeth Bisland, another family member and a journalist, became internationally known for her biography of Lafcadio Hearn, the noted journalist and author. Miss Bisland also achieved fame for her magazine articles in the *Ladies Home Journal*.

Descendants of William Bisland still occupy Mount Repose, which the Coyle Sessions Trust now owns. The house is open to the public during the Pilgrimages.

# Oakland

Horatio Eustis constructed Oakland in the late 1830s for his wife, Catherine Chotard. She was the granddaughter of Stephen (Don Esteban) Minor, the last governor of the Natchez district under Spanish rule. Mr. Minor hired Horatio Eustis, a Harvard graduate and a native of Rhode Island, as Catherine's tutor.

In 1858, Mr. Eustis sold the estate to his wife's cousin, John Minor, who was married to Katherine Surget of another prominent Natchez family. Descendants of the Minor family occupied Oakland until the late 1940s.

Distinguished by its fine architecture, this Greek Revival house is of brick construction. A full-length gallery with six square wooden columns and a wooden balustrade fronts the house. Two tall chimneys and three smaller chimneys project from the hipped roof. The classic mahogany entrance at the front features rectangular overhead lights.

Oakland's external appearance understates the massiveness of the interior. Inside, large rooms on both sides flank the wide center hall. These rooms boast ceilings of sixteen-and-one-half feet. Floor-to-ceiling windows bring maximum light and ventilation into the rooms. These windows have mahogany sashes and interior paneled shutters, which fold into a recess along their sides. The fireplace mantles are of plain, white marble, and Sheffield silver hardware enhances the solid mahogany interior doors. Other interior features are an impressive vaulted ceiling in the library and two large cisterns and an unusual "milk room" in the basement. A two-story brick building at the rear formerly was servants' quarters.

John Minor, who entertained lavishly during his time at Oakland, sympathized with the Union and welcomed its officers during the Civil War. Thus the house suffered no damage or loss during that trying time in Natchez. Today, Oakland is the home of Mr. and Mrs. Lawrence Adams and is open to the public during the spring Pilgrimage.

OAKLAND — DINING ROOM

OAKLAND — FRONT PARLOR

# The Parsonage

The reason behind the construction of The Parsonage is one of the more unusual legends of Natchez. Peter Little, the owner of Rosalie, made his fortune in the lumber business and married his young ward, Eliza, somewhat of a religious zealot. Her hospitality to any and all ministers of the church was constant and had reached the point where her somewhat less pious husband felt that his privacy was being invaded.

Thus, Mr. Little decided to build a suitable guest house just a short distance away so that his wife could welcome those seemingly ever-present preacher guests. The solution worked! Mrs. Little satisfied her religious fervor at The Parsonage, yet acted as the proper mistress of Rosalie. Just what Mr. Little wanted!

The Parsonage, built on a commanding site high on the bluffs overlooking the Mississippi, occupies part of what was once the parade grounds of Fort Rosalie. The solidly built brick house features a full basement floor, originally used as servants' quarters and kitchen. One reaches the four square-pillared pedimented front gallery by a large brick stairway just off Broadway Street. The entrance door, trimmed in classic Greek style, has stained-glass overhead- and side-lights. Instead of the usual columns, a recessed rear gallery features attractive brick arches. An additional bedroom wing was added to the house in the 1870s.

Entering from the front gallery, visitors step into a square reception hall with a formal parlor to the left and a large dining room behind the parlor. The elaborate furnishings include beautiful furniture, china, silver, and museum-quality accent pieces. These elaborate and interesting furnishings extend to the bedrooms as well.

Peter Little donated the house to the Methodist church, which sold the house in 1865. After passing through several owners, The Parsonage was acquired in 1893 by Mrs. James M. Metcalfe. Her descendants have occupied it ever since. The public can view the house during the spring Pilgrimage.

THE PARSONAGE — BEDROOM

THE PARSONAGE — PARLOR

THE PARSONAGE — LOWER-LEVEL DINING ROOM

# Ravenna

Built in 1835, Ravenna was one of the first Greek Revival–style homes in the area of Natchez. The two-story mansion features galleries recessed under the gable roof in both front and rear. One unusual feature of this mansion is the difference in its front columns: The six supporting the second-floor balcony feature Doric capitals; the six supporting the roof are capped in the Ionic order. Only the second-level balcony has a wooden balustrade around it.

William Harris, a planter, cotton broker, real estate developer, and city alderman, built Ravenna. Mrs. Harris, whose maiden name was Caroline Harrison, was the niece of President William Henry Harrison, the ninth president of the United States. President Harrison, who is remembered for his campaign slogan "Tippecanoe and Tyler too," served the shortest time of all U.S. presidents, dying a month after taking office.

The outstanding architectural feature of Ravenna's interior is its elliptical stairway in the central hallway. The curved railing of this stairway runs continuously, all the way to the attic. The front hallway also boasts a beautifully detailed arch with fluted columns supporting it on each side.

During the Civil War, Zuleika Metcalfe occupied Ravenna. Involved in smuggling supplies to the Southern forces, she became a Confederate heroine when Union troops, having discovered her activities, ousted her from her home.

Currently, Mrs. Catherine Brandon Morgan resides at Ravenna. The public can view this beautifully furnished home and its lovely gardens during the fall Pilgrimage. Many of Ravenna's shrubs and plantings remain from its earliest days.

# Richmond

Richmond, one of Natchez's most spacious homes, was built in three stages. The house's first stage dates back to the 1770s or 1780s. This original section, in the Spanish style and constructed of wood, had early additions of front and rear galleries. These additions obscure the original hand-hewn gutters, which collect rain water from the roof. Iron railings run alongside the exterior stairway, which rises from the ground to the second story. These railings also run between the square wooden pillars supporting the gallery roof. This exterior stairway and gallery, now at the right side of the house, were once the front of Richmond.

In 1832, Levin R. Marshall acquired the property. Within a short time, Mr. Marshall built a two-and-a-half-story Greek Revival addition, connected to the original Spanish-style building at a right angle. This new structure, which became the front of Richmond, features a raised portico at its entrance. Four fluted Ionic columns, set in pairs, support a pedimented roof projecting from the main gabled roof. A balustrade extends along the front of the house at the roof line; at each window an extended iron railing creates a small balcony.

The third addition, connected to the other end of the original Creole section in 1860, is a rather simply designed Georgian colonial structure built primarily to give the house more bedroom space.

After entering the house from the Greek Revival portico, visitors see a fifty-foot central hallway featuring classic ornaments, pillars, and a curving stairway lighted by a domed skylight. The hallway opens to double parlors on one side and to two bedrooms on the other. Double dining rooms stand in the oldest part of the house.

Levin Marshall's wealth included twenty-four-thousand acres of land in several states and more than eight hundred slaves. He also had business interests in New York. In Natchez he was president of the Commercial Bank, a principal in the Natchez Steam Packet Company, and a major stockholder in the Natchez Protective Insurance Company. Sam Houston awarded Mr. Marshall his Texas holdings because he financially supported the Texas Revolution. Reportedly, Marshall, Texas, is named for him.

An interesting story told about Mr. Marshall concerns the famous singer Jenny Lind, who visited Natchez in 1851. Because a severe winter storm prevented the promoters of Miss Lind's concert from unloading her piano from the river landing, Mr. Marshall loaned his grand piano to the "Swedish Nightingale."

Even though Mr. Marshall was a large slave holder, he sympathized with the Union cause and suffered severe losses during the Civil War. Eventually, he left his home and moved to New York.

Descendants of the Marshall family have always occupied Richmond, so much of the furniture and furnishings are original. The John Shelby Marshalls presently live in the house and graciously show it to the public during the spring Pilgrimage.

RICHMOND — BEDROOM

RICHMOND — PARLOR

#  Rosalie

Peter Little, a man of humble beginnings who had made his fortune in the lumber business, built Rosalie, an impressive Georgian mansion, in 1820. It's located on the bluff above Natchez-Under-the-Hill, on property that was once part of Fort Rosalie.

The square house, built of red brick, has a stately two-story portico at its front. The portico features four Doric columns, which support a second-floor gallery and a large pedimented projection with an oval window in its center. The front gallery walls are stuccoed white; at both levels, a wooden balustrade surrounds the galleries. Rear galleries also extend across the width of the house at both levels. Six large Doric columns support the rear galleries and roof.

At both the first- and the second-story level of Rosalie, the front and rear galleries feature similar doors with attractive fan- and side-lights. A white balustered widow's walk, or belvedere, tops the hipped roof of the square building. A single dormer projects from the rear roof.

The floor plan of Rosalie is fairly typical of other Natchez, nineteenth-century mansions: a large central hall with double parlors on one side, a library, stairway, and dining room on the other. A separate service building at the right rear of the house formerly contained a kitchen and servants' quarters.

According to local legend, Mr. Peter Little married his young ward, Eliza, who was orphaned by the death of her parents (his closest friends). Mr. Little sent Eliza to Maryland to be educated; she returned several years later to become the mistress of the mansion her older husband had built for her. Supposedly, Eliza enjoyed entertaining traveling ministers so frequently and Mr. Little so valued his privacy that he built and maintained a separate house nearby to accommodate her guests. The Parsonage, located across the street from Rosalie and described earlier in this text, is that house.

The Littles died childless, Eliza in 1853 and Peter in 1856, and the ownership of the property went to Mr. and Mrs. Andrew Wilson, who were their close friends. They furnished the house with a magnificent Belter parlor set, Mallard bedroom set, elegant mirrors, and several other pieces that visitors can still see.

Union troops occupied and used Rosalie as a headquarters during the Civil War. General Walter Gresham and his family occupied the house during that period, sharing it with and even becoming friends with Mrs. Wilson, who occupied the upper level. Reportedly, the general was most gracious in allowing Mrs. Wilson to preserve her furnishings intact. General Ulysses S. Grant was a guest in the house for a short time.

The Wilsons had no biological children, but they adopted children and their descendants remained at Rosalie until 1938. At that time, they sold the house to the Mississippi Society, Daughters of the American Revolution, who maintain and show Rosalie on a daily basis. Visitors to Rosalie enter its parklike grounds through a most attractive cypress picket fence painted white. Constructed without nails, the fence is made of slotted posts, slats, and pickets cleverly joined together.

ROSALIE — CHILDREN'S BEDROOM

ROSALIE — STAIRWAY

ROSALIE — PARLOR AND MUSIC ROOM

# Routhland

Job Routh built the original Routhland in about 1800 on land he had received by grant in 1792 from Baron Carondelet, the governor general of the territory. The "second Routhland" (the original burned to the ground), built by Job Routh's son, stands on a rise surrounded by eighteen acres of parklike grounds. Its Winchester Road location is near the heart of downtown Natchez.

The original structure consisted of a smaller house probably used as a summer house. Its expansion began in 1824, when John Routh, son of Job, received ten acres from his father's estate. In 1837, following a reversal of fortune, the Routh family auctioned off the property. A series of families owned it until 1871 when Charles Clark, an ex–Confederate general, acquired the house and grounds. (General Clark had served as governor of Mississippi during the Civil War.)

During his residency, General Clark remodeled and enlarged Routhland extensively. He is responsible for the curved front steps, which resemble open arms, a symbol of the hospitality of the house. The attractively designed steps lead to a wide front gallery, which has ten white Doric columns supporting its roof.

Routhland's interior features a center hall extending the length of the house with rooms opening onto each side. Visitors to this lovely home can view beautiful hand-crafted cypress doors, twelve-foot ceilings, woodwork with moldings of the egg-and-dart pattern, and marble mantles. The large double parlors are furnished with a mahogany parlor set original to the house. Other furnishings include a Waterford chandelier, an Aubusson carpet, Sheraton and Hepplewhite antiques, gold-leaf mirrors, and other museum-quality pieces.

Mr. and Mrs. Charles Ratcliffe occupy Routhland, which is owned by Mr. Ratcliffe and his sister, Mrs. Hector H. Howard. Her home—Rip Rap—is another of the many beautiful antebellum structures in Natchez. The Ratcliffes purchased the Routhland estate in the 1940s and began to restore the house shortly after. Visitors can view the attractive results of their efforts during the spring Pilgrimage when the Ratcliffes open their home to the public.

# Shields Town House

In 1860, Maurice Lisle constructed this town house. Mr. Lisle owned the Natchez Foundry, which installed the original natural gas system for the network of street lights in Natchez.

The Greek Revival house, one of the last to be constructed before the beginning of the American Civil War, features a front portico with four Doric columns. These fluted columns are mounted on Italianate pedestals between which carved balustrades engage the pedestals and the painted brick facade of the house. Rectangular top- and side-lights of umber etched glass, original to the house, enhance the front entrance.

The exterior of Shields Town House understates its spacious interior. A wide central hallway runs through the house, separating double parlors (one used as a dining room) on one side and a library and original master bedroom on the other. The double parlors feature matching King-of-Prussia marble mantles. Within the hallway, a stairway rises to a vaulted parlor and to guest rooms on the second level. The original rear gallery is now enclosed and utilized as a morning room with several large windows opening to an attractive courtyard.

In 1869, after the war, Wilmer Shields bought the property; it has been known as the Shields Town House ever since. (Mr. Shields owned Laurel Hill Plantation south of Natchez.) In 1978, Mr. and Mrs. William Samuel acquired the property and began a complete restoration of the house. The Perkins maintain a residence in the main house and offer the restored outbuildings for bed-and-breakfast guests.

Shields Town House is famous for its fine collection of mid-eighteenth- and early-nineteenth-century furnishings, paintings, and objects, which include fine Baltimore Hepplewhite, Philadelphia Sheraton, and Chippendale cabinets from the mid-eighteenth century.

The Shields Town House is on the National Register of Historic Places and has been shown on Pilgrimage tours since 1982.

SHIELDS TOWN HOUSE — SIDE GARDEN

SHIELDS TOWN HOUSE — BEDROOM

SHIELDS TOWN HOUSE — DINING ROOM

113

# Stanton Hall

Completed in late 1858, Stanton Hall is considered by many to be the most palatial house in Natchez. The estate occupies an entire city block, and the house is set on a knoll in the center of the site. An elaborate iron fence surrounds the entire property.

The style of Stanton Hall is an eclectic but harmonious blend of Greek Revival and Italianate architectural styles. At the front of the house, four enormous fluted columns, with oversized Corinthian capitals, support a second-floor gallery and a classic pedimented roof. Elaborate wrought-iron railings surround both the lower and the upper gallery. Black and white marble squares form the floor of the lower gallery, which visitors reach from granite stairs. The west side of the house features a pillared *porte-cochere* (a roof projecting over the driveway by the entrance); the east, a double verandah, trimmed in lacy ironwork.

Visitor to Stanton Hall enter the crescent-shaped drive through graceful wrought-iron gates and the house through a huge mahogany door, two-and-one-half inches thick, with silver doorknobs and hinges. The impressive doorway has inside-shuttered side-lights framed by smaller fluted columns.

Stanton Hall's interior dimensions are quite spacious: The central hallway (on both levels) measures sixteen feet wide and runs through the entire length of the seventy-foot-long main building. Ceilings on the first floor are more than sixteen feet tall. To the right of the central hall, a double parlor is divided by an elaborately carved, unsupported triple archway. A music room, located directly behind the parlors, features sliding doors. When these doors are open, they create a spacious ballroom, which appears even larger than it is because of massive French mirrors at each end. To the left of the central hall is the library, and behind that, a stair hall. The mahogany-railed stairway in this hall reaches up to the attic level. Visitors can enter the stair hall through the library, the central hall, or the *porte-cochere*.

Behind the stair hall is a dining room—a twenty-two- by forty-foot room with two white marble fireplaces set between floor-to-ceiling windows. Beyond the dining room are service rooms and servants' quarters. Stanton Hall has six bedrooms on the second floor with ceilings not quite as high as those on the lower level. It also has an attic, with a large cupola at its peak, and a smaller basement area below the main floor.

Frederick Stanton, whose family was of Irish aristocracy, emigrated from Ireland with his two brothers and settled in the Natchez area. He became a cotton broker and married Huldah Helm of the socially prominent and wealthy Helm family.

The Stantons lived at nearby Cherokee for a number of years, but Frederick Stanton wanted a more elaborate home, which, in his mind, would compare with his family estate in Ireland. He spared no expense. A trip to Europe resulted in his chartering an entire ship to bring to Natchez the huge French mirrors, Carrara marble fireplaces, bronze chandeliers, and silver hardware he purchased all over the continent to furnish his massive new mansion, which he originally named Belfast.

Sadly, the house, constructed by local craftsmen and artisans, was completed just a short time before Frederick Stanton died in 1859. His family remained there throughout the Civil War and into the 1890s. At that time, they leased it for use as a select girl's school. The school was called Stanton College,

and the property has been known as Stanton Hall ever since. In later years, the First Bank of Natchez seized the estate and sold it, reportedly for a fraction of the original cost, to Luther Childs, a restaurateur. In 1920, Mr. Childs sold the property to the Robert Clark family. Twenty years later, they sold it to the Pilgrimage Garden Club.

Since the 1940s, this palatial residence has been a preservation project of that noble organization, which furnished it with beautiful antiques and artifacts (some original to the house). Stanton Hall is open year-round to touring visitors, who can also view the attractively landscaped grounds from the famous Carriage House restaurant located at the rear of the property.

STANTON HALL — RED BEDROOM

STANTON HALL — DOUBLE PARLOR

# Texada

Built on property granted by the Spanish government to Don Miguel Solibellas on May 7, 1793, Texada was the first brick building in Natchez. Don Miguel constructed his home close to the street, on the corner of what is now known as Washington and Wall Street in the Old Spanish section of the city.

The building's name is derived from Don Manuel Garcia de Texada, who purchased it in 1798. Don Manuel, born in Castile, Spain, arrived in the Natchez area in the early 1780s. By the time of his death — in 1817 — Texada, a lawyer, tavern keeper, and planter, had bought and sold several plantations.

In 1817, Edward Turner purchased Texada. His career in public service included a stint as mayor of Natchez, attorney general of the state of Mississippi, speaker of the state House of Representatives, and chief justice of the state's Supreme Court.

Texada is a two-and-a-half-story structure with a steeply pitched roof, which is hipped on all but the north, gabled elevation. Dormers project from the hipped roof sections. A recessed Federal doorway, serving as its entrance, has a multipaned, semicircular fanlight above.

At the rear of the main building, separated by an attractive courtyard, stands a two-story building, which once served as a kitchen and servants' quarters but which is now part of a bed-and-breakfast complex owned and operated by Dr. and Mrs. George Moss, who also reside in the home.

Texada, recently restored, is beautifully furnished with American and English antiques and is open during the fall Pilgrimage for tours. During its lifetime, the house has been a residence, a tavern, a hotel, a place for the Mississippi legislature to meet, and a shop.

# Twin Oaks

Twin Oaks, a story-and-a-half cottage, is a charming example of an antebellum villa set in an old-fashioned garden. Lewis Evans, the sheriff of the Mississippi Territory, built the earliest section of the house about 1812. In 1820, Dr. Josiah Morris purchased it, but he died of yellow fever only three years later.

In 1832, Dr. Morris's widow and her second husband sold the estate to Pierce and Cornelia Connelly. Mr. Connelly was the rector of Trinity Episcopal Church in Natchez. The Connellys added the front house in the Greek Revival style and connected it to the original section with galleries.

Judge Charles Dubisson bought Twin Oaks for his bride in 1841. He served the Natchez area in several capacities, including that of president of nearby Jefferson College. After the death of his wife during a yellow fever epidemic and the death of a child who drowned in a cistern on the property, Judge Dubisson moved to Yazoo City and leased Twin Oaks during the Civil War. The Gastrell and Barton families owned the house from 1871 to 1940, when Dr. and Mrs. Homer Whittington purchased it and began its restoration. Known for more than a hundred years as White Cottage, the house's name was changed by Dr. Whittington to Twin Oaks to honor the massive live oaks that shade the house. Writers of its earliest land deeds used these oaks as landmarks.

Twin Oaks features a front portico with four tapered square pillars supporting its pedimented roof, which projects from the main gable roof. A half-round window provides light for a second-floor sitting area while two dormers illuminate the second-floor bedrooms. An unusual feature in the bedrooms is that the original closet openings are off the dormers.

Visitors enter the interior of Twin Oaks through a classic doorway with rectangular side- and fanlights. A walnut stairway in the central hall leads to the second floor. Double parlors and an original cabinet room stand on one side of the hall and two spacious bedrooms grace the other side. Having enclosed the rear gallery, Dr. Whittington utilizes it as a large family living room. A back hall joins the Greek Revival house to the dining wing, which was the original house.

Dr. and Mrs. Whittington have furnished Twin Oaks with an outstanding collection of American and European antiques, including magnificent tester beds; family heirlooms; Ginori china; and a Steinway grand piano made in 1876 for a German baroness living in New Orleans.

Twin Oaks is shown during the Pilgrimages, and the Whittingtons have a reputation for being as gracious as their home is beautiful.

# The Wigwam

This house, located near the corner of Oak and Myrtle streets, began as a large cottage, said to have been built in the middle 1790s. An eclectic blend of architectural styles, The Wigwam stands on property that was part of an eighteenth-century Spanish land grant.

Mr. and Mrs. Douglas Rivers remodeled The Wigwam's center section in 1856 and gave it its name — supposedly because the land on which it was located was once a Native American burial ground.

The Rivers' remodeling included projecting wings on each side of the original cottage building. These created an H-shaped structure. To the central portion of the house, the Rivers added Italianate features: cast-iron porch railings and posts, bracketed cornices, a large central dormer, and an unusual set of arched triple windows along each side of the formal doorway entrance. The remodeling also included balconies that extended around the added wings; however, later owners removed these.

Inside The Wigwam, visitors can view marble mantles, arched doorways, elegant plasterwork, and elaborate moldings. Historians attribute the painted ceiling in the ballroom to A. Conova, a well-known ornamental painter of the antebellum period.

During the Civil War, the Union army built Fort McPherson in the northern part of Natchez. At that time, Federal troops occupied The Wigwam, Cottage Gardens, Airlie, and The Burn, all of which were within the fort's boundaries.

Interestingly, the Myrtle Street neighborhood where The Wigwam stands was once an elegant Natchez suburb. Five governors of the Mississippi Territory and the state of Mississippi lived there.

The Wigwam's present owner, Estelle Madsey, operates the house as a bed-and-breakfast inn. It is open for tours all year.

THE BANKER'S HOUSE — PARLOR

# References

Brown, Dale C., Mary B. Eidt, Joan W. Gandy, and Carolyn V. Smith. 1977. *The Complete Guide to Natchez*. Natchez, MS: Myrtle Bank Publishers.

Brown, Dale C., Mary B. Eidt, Joan W. Gandy, and Carolyn V. Smith. 1977. *Stanton Hall*. Natchez, MS: Stanton Hall.

Callon, Sim C. and Carolyn Vance Smith. 1985. *The Goat Castle Murder*. Natchez, MS: Plantation Publishing.

Cooper, J. Wesley. 1957. *Natchez: A Treasure of Ante-Bellum Homes*. Philadelphia: Southern Historical Publications.

Crocker, Mary W. 1988. *Historic Architecture in Mississippi*. Jackson, MS: University Press of Mississippi.

Gleason, David K. 1982. *Plantation Homes of Louisiana and the Natchez Area*. Baton Rouge, LA: Louisiana State University Press.

Harris, Bill. 1987. *Grand Homes of the South*. New York: Crescent Books.

Kane, Harnett T. 1947. *Natchez on the Mississippi*. New York: Bonanza Books.

Kempe, Helen K.. 1977. *Pelican Guide to Old Homes of Mississippi*. Vol. 1, *Natchez and the South*. Gretna, LA: Pelican Publishing.

Miller, Mary Warren and Ronald W. Miller. 1986. *The Great Houses of Natchez*. Jackson, MS: University Press of Mississippi.

Sansing, David G., Sim C. Callon, and Carolyn V. Smith. 1992. *Natchez: An Illustrated History*. Natchez, MS: Plantation Publishing.

Schuler, Stanley. 1984. *Mississippi Valley Architecture: Houses of the Lower Mississippi Valley*. Exton, PA: Schiffer Publishing.

Smith, Reid and John Owens. 1969. *The Majesty of Natchez*. Gretna, LA: Pelican Publishing.

Smith, Carolyn V. 1984. *Secrets of Natchez*. Natchez, MS: Plantation Publishing.

Smith, J. Frazer. 1941. *White Pillars*. New York: Bramhall House.

Stuart, Jozefa and Wilson Gathings. 1977. *Great Southern Mansions*. New York: Walker Publishing.

Works Project Administration Federal Writers' Project. 1938. *Mississippi: A Guide to the Magnolia State*. New York: Viking.

# Index

# About the Authors

*Joseph Arrigo*

*Dick Dietrich*

New Orleans native Joseph Arrigo is the popular author of many books about the South, whose topics range from New Orleans to the Mississippi Gulf Coast to plantation homes in Louisiana. He is the author and illustrator of *Plantations: Forty-four of Louisiana's Most Beautiful Antebellum Plantation Homes* and *Louisiana's Plantation Homes: The Grace and Grandeur*. Arrigo is well-known for his award-winning drawings and illustrations. His work has been exhibited in many galleries and shows throughout the South. Arrigo continues to live and work in New Orleans.

For over thirty years, Dick Dietrich has been photographing landscapes and architecture all over the United States. He is a regular contributor to *Arizona Highways*, and his work has also been published in *National Geographic, Reader's Digest*, and other magazines. He is the author-photographer of *Arizona Postcard Collection*, and the photographer of *Louisiana's Plantation Homes: The Grace and Grandeur*. Dietrich lives in Phoenix.

Rudi Holnsteiner was born in 1941 in Steyr, Austria. He immigrated to the United States and has since enjoyed great success as a photographer, having exhibited his work in New York, Houston, Atlanta, and San Francisco. He has published photographs in *Mississippi Magazine, Readers' Digest International*, and *Americana Magazine*, as well as in Mississippi travel guides. He lives in Houston.